RAILS AROUND YORK AND THE VALE

COMPILED BY NICK DEACON IMAGES FROM THE NEVILLE STEAD COLLECTION

© Images and design Transport Treasury 2022 Text Nick Deacon

ISBN 978-1-913893-28-6

First published in 2023 by Transport Treasury Publishing Limited. 16 Highworth Close, High Wycombe, HP13 7PJ. Totem Publishing an imprint of Transport Treasury Publishing.

www.ttpublishing.co.uk

Printed in Tarxien, Malta By Gutenberg Press Ltd.

'*Rails around York and the Vale*' is one of books on specialist transport subjects published in strictly limited numbers and produced under the Totem Publishing imprint using material only available at The Transport Treasury.

Front Cover: The 10.00am ex-King's Cross 'Flying Scotsman' express emerges from the station canopy headed by immaculate Peppercorn A1 Pacific No. 60119 *Patrick Stirling* of King's Cross shed. The photograph, although undated, must be from the short period between September 1957 and August 1958 when the loco was at 'The Cross' before being moved to Doncaster shed. The loco honoured the name of the famous GNR loco designer, was completed in November 1948 and was only 15½ years old when withdrawn from Doncaster in May 1964. Although consistently reliable in service, free steaming and economic to maintain, the class were said to be rough-riding at higher speeds resulting in drivers being reluctant to run them as they would with A3 and A4 locos. That said, the class were the least troublesome of all the Doncaster Pacific breeds and of the three classes clocked up the greatest annual mileages. *NS204534*

Frontispiece: A magnificent pre-grouping portrait taken at York of one of the NER Class J 4-2-2 locos designed by T.W. Worsdell, the older brother of the more well-known NER loco engineer Wilson Worsdell. No. 1519 was built in November 1889 and was one of a class of ten 2-cylinder compound locos built for the Newcastle – Edinburgh express services on which they performed very creditably for some years. However, by 1894 Worsdell's successor, his brother Wilson, was not happy with their performance and the class was rebuilt as 2-cylinder 'simple' locos – No. 1519 receiving this treatment in January 1895. In their later careers, they were relegated to secondary services and No. 1519, while based at York, was used on fast commuter services to Leeds and Scarborough. In this 'post-compound' view taken near the 1839 water tank at York, the scorching of the smokebox door suggests an air leak, or an excessive char build-up but otherwise the loco is immaculate. It was withdrawn from Neville Hill shed, Leeds on 21st February 1920 having clocked up an estimated (and very respectable) 801,717 miles. *NS30003*

Back cover: Overlooked by the Royal Station Hotel on the east side of the station, LNER 3-cylinder Class B16/2 No. 61455 of York shed waits to leave with an early evening service (possibly the 5.16pm to Hull) on 20 June 1961. The train is about to leave the north end of the station but will turn south at Bootham Junction to join the Market Weighton line. The loco was completed in October 1923, one of the batch of 38 which appeared in 1924. A long-term York resident since 1934, it was rebuilt in November 1939 with the original three independent sets of Stephenson link motion replaced by two sets of Walschaerts gear to the outside valves with Gresley's derived motion to the inside valve. As such the loco was reclassified as 'B16/2' along with six others of the class oo modified in which form it ran until condemned from York in September 1963. She had received her last general overhaul over 145 days at Darlington between August and December 1960. *NS204546*

Introduction

The Vale of York lies in the centre of a predominantly low-lying area, rich in arable farmland drained by the River Ouse and its many tributaries. Lying between the Pennines in the west and the Howardian Hills and Yorkshire Wolds in the east, the area has been regarded since at least Roman times as the main north - south transport conduit for that part of northern England with York at its centre. In the pre-railway age the waterways took produce downstream to the Humber ports and busy coaching services plied along the best of the roads that criss-crossed the area with many of these, like the Roman Ermine Street, later becoming part of the modern network.

The first incursion of the railway into this topographically unchallenging area was the Leeds & Selby which received Royal Assent for its Bill in May 1830. In September 1834 the line was opened via Garforth and Milford to Selby at much the same time as the Hull & Selby Railway indicated its intention to apply for powers to extend the route into Hull. This line was duly opened in July 1840, but prior to this occurring another player had entered the lists – a controversial figure who was destined to loom large over the conduct of many railway boardrooms and their financial affairs.

'*Whereas the making of a Railway from the City of York to and into the Township of Altofts, and the making of several branches from the said Railway, all within the West Riding of the County of York or County of the same City, would be of public Advantage, by opening additional and expeditious Communications between the City of York and various Parts of the said West Riding, and also of the East Riding of the said County of York, and might also be the Means ultimately of effectuating the Establishment of a general expeditious line of Communication between the Northern Counties and the Midland and Western parts of England and the Metropolis.*' So ran the florid opening statement of the York and North Midland Railway (Y&NMR) Act dated 21st June 1836 which saw the arrival of George Hudson, later styled 'The Railway King', upon the stage of Britain's breakneck railway development.

At this time Hudson was already Lord Mayor of York and as Chairman of the Y&NMR with its HQ in the city he was able to consolidate his position over the next decade or so to become the driving force behind many of the railway schemes hatched in north-eastern England as well as chairing other railway companies such as the Midland, Newcastle & Berwick, Newcastle & Darlington Junction, and the Eastern Counties Railway companies.

In April 1837, work started on the southern route of the Y&NMR from York to Church Fenton and thence to join the Leeds & Selby Railway at Milford Junction. To coincide with the arrival of the Great North of England Railway from Darlington and Thirsk, a new joint terminal station replacing the 1839 temporary station *outside* the city walls was opened *within* the York city walls in 1841. This remained in use until June 1877 when it was replaced by the magnificent through station built by the NER and placed *outside* the city walls thus avoiding the need to reverse passenger services at the old terminal. Two other Y&NMR lines opened from York during Hudson's chairmanship: firstly the Scarborough line via Malton in July 1845 and secondly the first section of the Beverley line as far as Market Weighton in October 1847. The remaining section to Beverley was delayed by the collapse of

Hudson's empire and the ensuing unfavourable financial climate until 1865. In October 1851, after some delay caused by the collapse of the bridge over the River Nidd, the East & West Yorkshire Junction Railway (E&WYJR) reached Knaresborough from York and made an end-on junction with the Leeds & Northern Railway branch from Starbeck. Harrogate had already been reached, albeit circuitously, by the Y&NMR via Church Fenton and Wetherby in 1848, but it was not until 1862 that the town was graced by a central station built by the North Eastern Railway (NER) and the line extended eastwards to permit through traffic to York via the former E&WYJR route.

The last main line section to open within the remit of this book was the northern section of the NER's line from Doncaster via Selby to Chaloners Whin Junction 2 miles south of York on the Church Fenton Line. This opened in 1871 and became part of the East Coast Main Line until BR opened a 14½ mile diversionary route to the west in 1983 with this coming off the Church Fenton line at Colton five miles south of York. Just to the north of Naburn, the original line crossed the River Ouse on a swing bridge consisting of two wrought-iron bowstring spans - one fixed span of 108ft in length and the swing span section of 180ft.

Also falling within the orbit of this book are two standard gauge light railways: the 2½ mile Easingwold Light Railway opened in July 1891 from a junction on the Thirsk line at Alne and the 16 mile Derwent Valley Light Railway opened throughout in July 1913 from Layerthorpe near York to Cliffe Common on the Selby to Market Weighton line. Given that York occupies the main focal point of this book, also of interest are the lines mentioned above which, like the spokes of a wheel, radiate from its epicentre and their inclusion within this work adds an extra dash of flavour to an already diverse mix. Obviously space limits the amount of attention given to the latter and so coverage of each extends up to a 'stop point' viz: Thirsk, Malton, Market Weighton, Selby, Church Fenton, and Harrogate. These routes, with selected and named photographic locations, are shown with thicker lines on the map.

The 'steam age' images contained herein are largely those taken during the 1950/60's BR period but also with a sprinkling of pre-1948 and pre-1923 shots for added flavour. It is hoped the selection goes some way to reflect the rich and diverse trackside sights which could be seen regularly in the area covered by the book before being swept away by the cull of dieselisation.

With thanks to members of the North Eastern Railway Association (NERA).

Special thanks to Neville Stead for his memories which have enhanced many of the captions.

Sources consulted:
North Eastern Locomotive Sheds. Ken Hoole. David & Charles 1972.
Rail Centres: York. Ken Hoole. Ian Allan. 1983.
RCTS Locomotives of the LNER. Various editions.
The North Eastern Railway. Cecil J. Allen. Ian Allan 1964.
Various archive periodicals e.g. British Railways Illustrated, Steam Days etc.
The 6 Bells Junction website.
Various editions of the *Railway Observer* through the years.

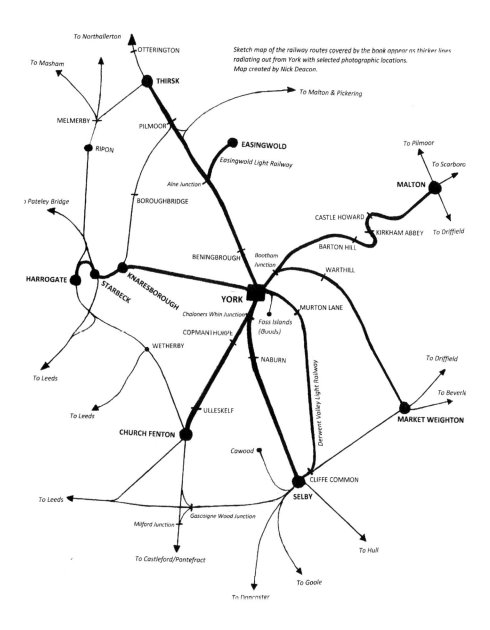

To Northallerton
OTTERINGTON
To Masham
THIRSK

Sketch map of the railway routes covered by the book appear as thicker lines radiating out from York with selected photographic locations. Map created by Nick Deacon.

To Malton & Pickering

MELMERBY
PILMOOR
RIPON
EASINGWOLD
Easingwold Light Railway

To Pilmoor
To Scarboro

Alne Junction
MALTON

> Pateley Bridge
BOROUGHBRIDGE

CASTLE HOWARD
KIRKHAM ABBEY   To Driffield

BENINGBROUGH   Bootham Junction
BARTON HILL

HARROGATE   KNARESBOROUGH   WARTHILL
STARBECK
YORK
Chaloners Whin Junction   MURTON LANE
COPMANTHORPE   Foss Islands (Goods)
WETHERBY

To Leeds   NABURN
To Driffield

To Leeds   ULLESKELF
To Beverle

CHURCH FENTON   Cawood
MARKET WEIGHTON

Derwent Valley Light Railway

To Leeds   CLIFFE COMMON
SELBY
Milford Junction   Gascoigne Wood Junction

To Castleford/Pontefract   To Hull
To Goole
To Doncaster

Opposite: At the south end of the station opposite the carriage shed, a sparkling pairing of Class X3 2-2-4T No. 1679 with ex-NER bogie clerestory inspection saloon carriage No. 305. (now numbered 2305 by the LNER) The loco was one of two Class 190s built by the NER as 'Officers' Special Tank Engines' for the haulage of inspection saloons. Remarkably, No. 1679 had started life as a three-cylinder 4-2-0 tender engine emerging from Robert Stephenson's Works in 1846. It was rebuilt to a 2-2-2 in 1853, then a two cylinder 2-2-2 in 1860 with a further rebuild in 1884 before finally becoming a 2-2-4T in October 1894 and renumbered from 77 to 1679. Although built for a specific departmental purpose, the loco occasionally worked revenue earning traffic in the years before the Great War and it also hauled the first DVLR passenger train on 19th July 1913. The loco appears to have been based solely at York and worked there until withdrawn in June 1931 when it was replaced by its classmate No. 190 transferred from Heaton shed. The Diagram 81 saloon carriage No. 2305 dated from 1903, became No. E902177E/99051 which survived to be restored and preserved as NER No. 305 with the restoration work carried out by British Rail Engineering Limited (BREL) York in 1973. The vehicle later spent time at the Ribble Steam Railway before becoming part of the 'One:One Collection' of preserved railway stock based at Margate, Kent. Also of note is the shunter riding on the footboard and breaking all the rules! *NS202208*

Top: Appropriately for the location, Vincent Raven's NER 3-cylinder Class A2 Pacific No. 2402 *City of York* displays its impressive proportions to good effect, probably after August 1934 when it had been transferred to York from Gateshead. The other four members of the class made similar moves by the end of the year and all remained at York until withdrawn during 1936/7. The class was said to have been a 'stretched' version of Raven's superheated Class Z (LNER Class C7) Atlantic design intended for the increased loadings of the Anglo-Scottish expresses plying between York and Edinburgh. All five were in service by March 1924 and named after cities exclusively served by the NER. Unfortunately, although the class performed adequately enough 'on the road', they offered no marked improvement over the Atlantic locos and their fate was ultimately sealed with the appearance of the Doncaster-built A1/A3 Pacifics which became the standard LNER express loco. Comment at the time of the appearance of the five A2s suggested that the design had been 'rushed' with much being sacrificed in order for the company to achieve a Pacific in service before its independence disappeared with the 1923 Grouping. No. 2402 was completed in March 1924 and withdrawn in July 1936. *NS202003*

Bottom: The Great Central had a penchant for impressive, shapely locos and their six-strong Class I named 4-6-0s introduced between 1912/13 were certainly within that category. Reclassified by the LNER as 'B2' and later 'B19', No. 5424 *City of Lincoln* was photographed at York (probably at one of the 'South' sheds) during the 1930s when fetchingly turned out with the LNER passenger lined green livery. After 1936 until 1942 she was appropriately based at Lincoln and regularly hauled the York portion of the Harwich Boat Train. Although the steaming abilities of the class were said to be 'limited' they were adequate performers when not overtaxed and lasted until the mid to late 1940s when all six were based at Immingham shed. No. 5424 departed this life in November 1945. *NS202506*

From their first appearance in 1919, York became synonymous with the NER 3-cylinder Class S3 mixed traffic 4-6-0s designed by Vincent Raven. Completion of the class of seventy in 1924, and reclassification by the LNER as 'B16', saw York with an allocation of 28 – a figure which hardly changed during the 1930s and indeed, during WW2 and a little after, increased to include the entire class so as to concentrate maintenance and spare parts. The RCTS 'Green Guide' Part 2B commented that they were most versatile machines and worked with reliability whatever class of train was entrusted to them. One could even say that like the proverbial milkman's horse they could have found their way back to York unaided! Looking suitably imposing awaiting departure with a passenger stopper service, No. 1408 was one of the first of the class completed in April 1920 and numbered 848 but now carries her LNER December 1946 number prior to this changing under BR in December 1949 to 61477. Unlike many of her classmates she was never rebuilt to 'B16/2' or 'B16/3' and received her last general overhaul at Darlington at the end of 1955 which served until withdrawal from York on 1st February 1960. Regrettably, none of the class was preserved. *NS201408*

At the south end of the station in 1946 there's not much pomp on show but plenty of immediate post-war grime and visible damage to the station canopies inflicted by the 29th April 1942 'Baedeker' air raid. The same raid hit York North shed resulting in the withdrawal of the badly damaged A4 Pacific No. 4469 *Sir Ralph Wedgwood* and B16 4-6-0 No. 925. A war-weary Grantham-based A4 No. 4498 *Sir Nigel Gresley* awaits departure with a southbound express and is flanked by an equally weary A3 Pacific – shedmate No. 2555 *Centenary* heading a Class C parcels service. Matters improved the following year with both locos receiving general overhauls and reappearing with fresh liveries – No. 4498 in Garter blue and numbered '7' and No. 2555 in LNER apple green numbered '56'. *NS206303*

Away from the glamour of the main line heavyweights, tiny ex-NER Class K (LNER Class Y8) 0-4-0T No. 8091 lurks inside one of the York North roundhouses in the immediate post-nationalisation period. The loco was built at Gateshead Works in June 1890 and was one of a small class of five designed by T.W. Worsdell for use within the tight track curvatures of Hull docks. The meagre coal capacity of 4cwt was invariably supplemented by the means seen in the photograph. Three of the class were scrapped between 1936-7, but in May 1943 No. 8091 (then numbered No. 560) was moved to York to replace classmate No. 559 on shed pilot duties. At York it acquired vacuum brake equipment in order to move similarly fitted locos around the shed premises and also gained the affectionate nickname 'The Pup'. This most useful loco was said to have been 'worth its weight in gold', managing to survive until November 1956 when a cracked cylinder, a condemned boiler, and a lack of spares spelled its doom. Prior to this it had been withdrawn from normal stock in June 1954 to become 'Departmental Locomotive 55'. It never carried its BR allocated number '68091'. *NS205000*

Two Southern Railway ex-LB&SCR B4 4-4-0s, Nos. 2051/68, were recipients of an unexpected odyssey which in November 1941 took them out of store at Southern Railway sheds, steamed and moved to Leeds Neville Hill shed for a loan period. Until their return south in December 1944 both engines were based at York and used on Hull, Harrogate, Leeds, and Selby services and also for piloting work on heavy east coast express services. Now looking very tired, No. 2068 is seen at York - probably towards the end of her northern sojourn. Both locos were in good condition on their arrival in the North-East and apparently clocked up some 40,000 miles apiece during their first eighteen months. Afterwards however, lack of maintenance and continual heavy work took its toll and on their return south both were found to be worn out and never worked again. No. 2068 (old L&BSCR No. 68 formerly named *Marlborough*) was stored at Eastbourne shed, languishing there until finally withdrawn in June 1951 whilst No. 2051 (old L&BSCR No. 51 formerly named *Wolferton*) had already been disposed of from Horsham shed in March 1949. *NS204680A*

A 1947/8 shot of LNER Class C7 Atlantic No. 2954 (ex-NER No. 716) passing Chaloners Whin Junction with a Class F coal empties duty - possibly from Scarborough where she was based at this time. Built in July 1911, she was one of the 50 Vincent Raven 3-cylinder Class Z introduced between 1911 and 1918 for express duties. The design was intended as a development of the Worsdell 2-cylinder Class R 4-4-0s (LNER Class D21) but in practice had much more in common with the Worsdell Class V Atlantic locos introduced between 1903 – 10. In service the new class proved successful enough although they quickly acquired a reputation for being poor hill climbers, needing double heading on certain services. During the 1930s the availability of Pacifics plus V2 2-6-2s saw the C7s increasingly relegated to secondary duties and but for the intervention of WW2, withdrawal of the class would have commenced earlier than it did. The last fourteen of the class were withdrawn during 1948 including No. 2954 going from Scarborough shed in June. *NS201677*

The original GNER/Y&NMR terminus station looking north-east as seen from the eminence of the city walls in 1962. Forming the backdrop in ascending order are a new office block spanning the tracks, the 1853 hotel and lastly the splendid edifice of the NER 1906 offices with a roof-mounted aerial for BR communications. The station was designed by G.T. Andrews who was closely associated with Hudson's stations as well as those for the GNER. The station opened initially for mineral traffic on 4th January 1841 (and for passengers by July) and originally comprised a collection of pitched roofs covering the various platform bays, but by the date of the photograph only one of the roofs has survived. Once the new station had opened in 1877 the terminus was relegated to stabling carriage and van stock although occasionally it was used for excursion and 'special event' passenger traffic. By 1966 the station was surplus to requirements and demolition commenced during the same year with the site subsequently cleared for the new BR Eastern Region HQ building of Hudson House – this suffered the same fate in 2018! *NS204502*

Controversially, Hudson wanted to bring the Y&NMR into the heart of the city which meant breaching the ancient city walls, but in such a way as to reinstate the sacrosanct walkway along the crest of the wall. A plan by G.T. Andrews was accepted which sympathetically inserted a Tudor-style archway allowing a two-track approach to the station throat. Posed under the arch whilst shunting carriage stock on 16 June 1951 is long-term York resident Class J71 0-6-0T No. 68246, a veteran from July 1889 and regularly seen on pilot and shunting duties in the immediate area. The loco was occasionally loaned out with other members of the class to the Easingwold Railway when it was temporarily bereft of its single loco and also on one occasion powered an RCTS open wagon special along the line on 23rd June 1957. No. 68246 lasted at York until withdrawn in November 1958. *AF0246*

Witnessed by a bevy of excited young 'spotters sometime in the late 1950s/very early 1960s, the 9.30am non-stop King's Cross – Edinburgh Waverley *The Elizabethan* express coasts through the north end of York station headed by long-term Haymarket shed A4 Pacific No. 60011 *Empire of India*. The train appeared from May 1948 as *The Capitals Limited* but was rechristened in 1953 to honour the crowning of Elizabeth II. The train ran during the summer months from June until September and covered the 393 mile distance in approximately 6 hours 30 minutes averaging 60mph to arrive in Edinburgh at around 4pm. Two through coaches for Aberdeen were also included. At the time it was the longest scheduled non-stop railway journey in the world, and such was the pride in working the train it was rare that any time was lost by Kings Cross men. No. 60011 received a double chimney in January 1958 and lasted at Haymarket until June/July 1962 when it was transferred to Aberdeen Ferryhill shed to work the 3 hour expresses to Glasgow. The loco returned south to Darlington allegedly for a repair in May 1964 but was deemed too far gone, was condemned later that month, and broken up during February 1965. Steam haulage on the express lasted until September 1961 when it was replaced by 'Deltic' power until the service finished in 1962. The express was famously recorded in a 20 minute British Transport Film shot over a few weeks in 1954. *NS204533.*

From July 1958 when unnamed LMS Patriot 4-6-0 No. 45517 had arrived at Bank Hall shed initially on loan from Willesden shed, the loco was employed on a wide variety of cross-country passenger turns including a regular appearance at York with services from Liverpool Exchange. She became a permanent and much favoured resident at Bank Hall from November 1958 and is seen south of York passing Dringhouses reception sidings sometime in the late 1950s/early 1960s with a service from Liverpool. Unlike some of her classmates, the loco was never rebuilt and remained in original condition until withdrawn from Bank Hall in June 1962 having achieved a mileage just shy of 1,329,000. She disappeared into 'The Melts' at Crewe Works the following month. *NS204527*

Worsdell Class J72 0-6-0T No. 68735 carries out pilot duties at the south-east side of York station sometime in the mid-1950s. One of the lamps on the front frame would have shown a red lens indicating the loco was on station pilot/shunting duties – not as it might seem a Class A express service! At around this time the loco was one of around ten of the class at York with five employed on station pilot duties at the South Up and Down sides, the Scarborough side, the North Down side and Clifton carriage sidings. Until May 1961 steam pilot locos were stabled at one of the South shed roundhouses. By the end of 1961 the J72s had disappeared from their traditional roles at York having been gradually replaced by 350hp shunters and, most surprisingly, the arrival of five ex-LMS 3F 'Jinty' 0-6-0Ts at different times between 1957-9. No. 68735 was a long-term York resident and remained there until withdrawn in October 1958. NS204512

The Holgate Excursion station had opened in December 1860 to serve York Racecourse but was last used in that capacity just prior to the outbreak of WW2. However, it remained accessible, and the Up platform became a favoured spot for railway photography for many years. In this view from the location looking north towards the 1911 Holgate Road girder bridge, a typically smart King's Cross shed 3-cylinder Class V2 No. 60814 heads for home with an express in 1956. At around this time York shed had thirty of these highly regarded and versatile locos for a variety of duties – an allocation which by 1961 had actually increased to thirty-three and there were still twelve on the books at the beginning of 1965 when steam was nearing its end. No. 60814 moved to Grantham in June 1962 and was withdrawn from there in April 1963. *NS204522*

Looking south from Holgate in July 1954, Gresley Class D49 4-4-0 No. 62739 *The Badsworth* passes with a Class F mineral freight from Gascoigne Wood marshalling yard to Scarborough. The marshalling yard was just east of Gascoigne Wood Junction on the Leeds – Selby line and was a concentration point for coal workings from local collieries. This particular service was one of the few allowed to pass through York station in order to access the Scarborough line north of the station. Completed in May 1932, the loco was one of a class of seventy-six 3-cylinder locos designed for express passenger work. Forty-eight were named after 'Hunts' operating largely within LNER territory. During the 1930s many were allocated to York for main line services to Newcastle, and cross-country services to Hull, Sheffield, Grantham, and Lincoln plus from time to time excursion services to King's Cross, but by the 1950s most had been cascaded to lesser duties as seen here. No. 62739, a Scarborough shed loco at the time of the photograph, remained there until withdrawn in October 1960. *NS204538*

Also seen passing Holgate is ex-LMS Fairburn Class 4MT 2-6-4T No. 42139 leaving York with a Leeds-bound service in the mid-1950s. The loco was based at Bradford Manningham shed and was regularly seen on this service before moving north of the border in 1960. It had been built at Derby in March 1950 and spent its first four years based at Kentish Town working London suburban services until moving to Manningham in November 1954. It returned south to Leeds Holbeck shed in April 1964 and was withdrawn from there in December 1965. Of interest is the mixed nature of the coaching stock with the first three steel angled trussed vehicles behind the loco dating to the LNER Gresley period - one of which (the brake) retains its varnished teak finish and the other two having received the BR carmine and cream livery. The remainder of the train includes two BR Mk 1 vehicles plus others lost in the smoke. *NS204519*

York was often host to the ex-LMS Garratt 2-6-6-2T locos based at Hasland, Toton and Wellingborough sheds for working the Teesside iron ore trains from Wellingborough. Often the locos would work through to Middlesbrough but in this undated scene from the mid-1950s No. 47977 has come off the train at York and will return to Wellingborough with the empties. Completed by Beyer, Peacock Ltd in September 1930, the loco was one of thirty-three of the class built between 1927 and 1930 for working heavy coal and iron ore trains. Although successful in this role the locos did not age well, suffering from high maintenance overheads plus their great length (nearly 88ft!) limited their availability. At sheds where allocated they also needed dedicated extra length accommodation 'roads'. With the availability of the BR Standard Class 9F 2-10-0 locos in the 1950s the last of the class had been withdrawn in 1958. No. 47977, seen at York North shed, was withdrawn from Hasland in June 1956. *NS203929*

Hawksworth's GWR 'Modified Hall' 4-6-0 No. 6979 *Helperly Hall* was built in 1947 and spent its entire career at Banbury shed before being withdrawn in February 1965. Flanked by York's A1 Pacific 60153 *Flamboyant* and Black 5 4-6-0 No. 45315 from Carlisle Upperby shed, the loco is seen at York North shed on Sunday 23rd August 1959 having brought in the 11.16am ex-Bournemouth West-York service the previous day. There were difficulties on the trip due to delays caused by a derailment at Leicester and No. 6979 needing a pilot from Nottingham - all of which resulted in a three hour plus late arrival at York. The Hall spent the rest of the weekend at York and returned south on Monday 24 August on the 5.30am York Dringhouses - Cardiff freight. Also of interest is a Class K1 2-6-0 (York's No.62061?) minus a set of wheels stabled 'off-shed' on a siding on the other side of the running lines. What was going on here? *NS208405*

Until the mid-1930s York had a substantial allocation of Wilson Worsdell's very successful NER 2-cylinder Class R 4-4-0s (LNER Class D20) which were introduced from 1899. However, with the appearance of the LNER D49 4-4-0s the legendary 4-4-0s began to be cascaded to second line duties and to sheds such as Alnmouth, Selby and Starbeck. By December 1947 York had just a handful of the class remaining- one of them a very well-cared for No. 62369 seen here in a captivating portrait taken at the south end of York on 10 June 1950 in company with Neville Hill B1 4-6-0 No. 61339. However, the loco was not destined to remain at York for much longer as it was moved to Starbeck shed in September where it was withdrawn in March 1951. *NS201587*

On 1st July 1951 York saw the last visit of No. 50455, the sole surviving member of the L&YR 'Dreadnought' 4-6-0s, hauling a railway society (SLS/MLS) special from Blackpool via Manchester to York and back to mark the last occasion the class would haul a passenger train. The loco was the first of twenty numbered 10455-74 built at Horwich by the LMS during 1924-25 originally intended to be 'Dreadnought Tank' 4-6-4Ts but as the LMS did not favour large tank locos the frames were altered for use as 'Dreadnought' 4-6-0s. No.10455 was the only one of the six post-1948 survivors numbered into BR stock and latterly had been confined to freight duties based at Blackpool shed. The 11-coach special is seen at the south end of York station awaiting its 6.15pm departure for Blackpool. Although the loco had recently received a general repair at Horwich and had been specially cleaned for the occasion, during the run it 'knocked' badly and on the return leg ran hot which prevented fast running resulting in a late arrival. Once back in Blackpool it saw little use and was withdrawn on 6th October 1951. *NS203984*

Dapper LMS Stanier 'Jubilee' 4-6-0 No. 45572 *Eire* of Bristol Barrow Road shed has an admiring audience of one young chap as it awaits departure in the mid – to late 1950s with possibly the 12.50pm ex-Newcastle to Bristol Temple Meads service. The train has been brought in probably by a Gateshead-based A3 Pacific and replaced by the Jubilee which will continue the journey south. Barrow Road's stud of six or seven of the class ranged far and wide on cross-country services and were regularly seen at York until finally displaced in the Spring of 1964. The loco, built in September 1934, moved from Barrow Road to Shrewsbury in October 1961 and was withdrawn from Willesden shed in January 1964. *NS204515*

A scene which for many will be a vivid reminder of their 'spotting days when rookeries of youthful 'platform-enders' were a common sight at major stations. Although some station authorities discouraged or even banned such gatherings, this little community seen at York on 19th August 1961 clearly had no fear of being 'cleared off' providing that common sense and good behaviour prevailed. Completing the nostalgic tableau is Britannia Pacific No. 70003 *John Bunyan* from March shed heading a 3.15pm departure for Colchester. The 'Brit' was one of the GE allocation demoted from Norwich shed from early 1961 as a result of main line dieselisation. No. 70003 had arrived at March in July 1961 and was used on a variety of 'out and back' services including the 7.17am Colchester-Newcastle due at York at 1.45pm. On one occasion it was even seen at Scarborough! The loco moved to Carlisle Kingmoor shed in December 1963 and remained there until withdrawn in March 1967. *JH2889*

On 22nd August 1959 LMS Class 4F 0-6-0 No. 44207 from Leeds Stourton shed and a Class J39 0-6-0 (probably No. 64824 of Gorton shed returning home) pass North shed engine yard most unusually double heading the Class C Heaton – Manchester Red Bank Carriage Sidings empty van train. The outward nocturnal working was mainly newspaper traffic from the presses of the Manchester newspaper world and rarely photographed, but the daylight returns to the city with twenty or more vans hauled by a variety of locos became favoured photographic subjects in steam days. The make-up of this particular train seen on this occasion was a typical mix of stock with at least three Southern Railway 'PMV' utility vans, three BR Mk 1 carriages and an LNER Thompson-era steel-bodied vehicle. The service remained doggedly steam-hauled until 1967.
NS208396

Enclosed by York's magnificent train shed roof, LNER Peppercorn Pacific No. 60128 *Bongrace* of King's Cross shed is positioned under the projecting water feed gantry at platform 9 with a northbound express on 1st May 1958. Thomas Prosser, the NER architect until his retirement in 1874, and the company's chief engineer, Thomas Harrison, are credited with the lion's share of the station design, although William Bell, who became the company's architect in 1877, also made a significant contribution. After an initial hiatus involving the first appointed contractor, John Keswick of York, the contract was rescinded and awarded to the London contractors, Lucas Brothers, at a price of £187,468 with an additional £30,626 set aside for engineering work. When opened in 1877, the station had 13 platforms covered by four glazed train shed spans, the largest of these being 81ft wide, 48ft high and 800ft long covering four central tracks. A 55ft span (40ft high) was shouldered against each side of the main span with an additional 43ft span (36ft high) added to the north and south sides of the main station building. The station was awarded a Grade II listing in 1968. *NS204544*

The classic view of the north end of York station with A3 Pacific No. 60072 *Sunstar* of Tweedmouth shed departing with a Bristol – Newcastle express on 21st May 1959. The carriage stock includes an LNER-era restaurant car amongst the BR Mk1 vehicles. Seen above the train is the imposing Royal Station Hotel completed in 1878. Although No. 60072 is in grubby condition (Tweedmouth, like most of the Newcastle area sheds, was never renowned for the external cleanliness of its locos), it nevertheless looks in good fettle as it gets up speed for the journey north. Completed during September 1924 and named after the winner of the 1911 Derby and 2,000 Guineas races, it had arrived at Tweedmouth from Heaton shed during September 1958 accompanied by classmate No. 60069 *Sceptre* from the same shed. The two were the only A3s ever allocated there, and both remained until transferred to Leeds Copley Hill during June 1960. While at Tweedmouth both received double chimneys - *Sunstar* in July 1959 with *Sceptre* following in September. After time at Copley Hill and then Leeds Holbeck sheds, No. 60072 returned to Heaton shed (where she had been based from 1943 until the move to Tweedmouth) where withdrawal occurred on 22 October 1962 – coincidentally the same month as No. 60069 was also condemned. *NS204548*

At the south end of the station in August 1955, WD 2-8-0 No. 90091 of Newport shed (Darlington District) pauses with a Class F unfitted train of bolster wagons loaded with steel from Teesside. The loco emerged from the North British Loco Co., Glasgow in October 1944 and spent the majority of its career in the North-East before moving to its last shed at Goole in November 1963 where it was condemned in June 1967. Newport and Middlesbrough sheds closed on 1st June 1958 and the locos from both (including No. 90091) were transferred to the new Thornaby shed.

A total of 935 of the Riddles-designed class were built between 1943-5 as a response to the rail transport needs of WW2. Somewhat unloved by the railway authorities and enthusiasts alike, nevertheless the 'Dub-Dee' type steamed well and proved to have a brute pulling power although it was hardly a comfortable steed to ride if speeds got above plodding rate. During the latter days of British steam when maintenance became threadbare the WD was able to soldier on in the most challenging circumstances and so it was no surprise the type survived into 1967 when the last 123 members including No. 90091 were withdrawn. *NS207800*

Grouped around one of the two roundhouse turntables in York North shed are three BR Riddles Class 9F 2-10-0s which had all arrived during September 1963. Nos. 92005/6 were from Newport Ebbw Junction shed whilst No. 92239 had arrived from Feltham shed on the Southern Region. Other members of the class, Nos. 92211/21, had arrived at much the same time. Soon after their arrival the locos were put to work on heavy freight duties and on the regular Dringhouses to Woodford Halse duty they replaced B1, B16 and V2 locos formerly diagrammed for the job. Although undated, the photograph may have been taken soon after the arrival of the class at York. Ivatt LMS 4MT 2-6-0 No. 43055 had arrived with six others of the class in October/November 1959 and it stayed until transferred away in December 1965. *NS204530*

An unusual interior view of York North roundhouse shed which after remodelling in 1957-8 contained the former No. 3 and 4 roundhouses under one roof but still grouped around their respective 60ft and 70ft turntables. On 6 July 1963 two visitors stride past from left to right, K1 2-6-0 No. 62057, an Ivatt LMS 4MT 2-6-0, K1 No. 62009, a V2 2-6-2 and B1 No. 61031 *Reedbuck*. Glimpsed to the left of the B1 is BR Standard 3MT 2-6-0 No. 77013 stabled on one of the roads of the 'straight' shed erected in place of roundhouses Nos. 1 and 2 in 1957-8. All the identified locos were allocated to York at the date of the photograph. In December 1966 York had the melancholy distinction of seeing its last V2, No. 60831, condemned. The loco was also the last of the class to work in England and with its passing York's unbroken association with the class stretching back to August 1936 was broken. *NS204531A*

The York North 500-ton capacity concrete coaling tower with four chutes was built by Mitchell Engineering Co., London to one of their own designs for £8,073 and installed ready for use in 1932. In 1948 LMS Stanier 'Black 5' 4-6-0 No. 5226 from Bank Hall shed is under the chutes about to take on victuals accompanied by York's Class J21 0-6-0 No. 5068. After the closure of the shed to steam in 1967 the coaling plant was demolished (with some considerable difficulty) in 1970. The J21 dated from December 1890 and was soon to move to Selby and then Darlington where it was withdrawn in June 1954 whilst the 'Black 5' moved between various LMR sheds and finished its career at Lostock Hall in September 1967. *NS204513*

At the south end of York station there were eventually five loco sheds – three roundhouses and two 'straight' buildings which were all 'subbed' as 'York South' to North shed when this was opened in 1878. Until demolished in 1963, one of the roundhouses was the second of a group of three built successively in 1850, 1851/2 and 1864 and used in later years (until 1961) as a stabling point for the station pilots and afterwards to store side-lined locos. Within the now roofless roundhouse, two of the station pilots, Worsdell J72 0-6-0T No. 68677 and one of the LMS Fowler 3F 0-6-0T Interlopers, No. 47334, form an interesting tableau around the 42ft turntable on 20th September 1959. The J72 was a long-term York resident until withdrawn in October 1961 while the 3F had arrived in December 1958 and stayed until moved to Hull Dairycoates shed in February 1960. *NS208492*

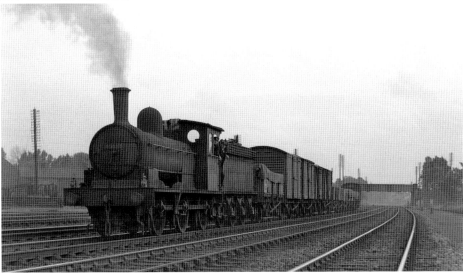

Worsdell J25 0-6-0 No. 65683 dated from November 1899 and the old warhorse is seen on a 'bread and butter' local transfer/trip duty near Chaloners Whin Junction. By now carrying a York (50A) shedplate, the photograph possibly dates from the loco's final period of service from July 1957 when it had returned to York after periods at Selby and Neville Hill sheds. The class began to be displaced at York during the 1950s by the arrival of Ivatt and BR Standard 2-6-0s and accordingly No. 65683 was condemned on 2nd June 1958 and broken up at Darlington. Although the loco appears to be carrying express lamps on the front frame, one would be showing a red lens indicating the train was on a transfer/trip duty. Lacking a brake van, the guard accompanies the crew on the footplate. *NS204526*

A memorable visitor to York was 'The East Midlander No. 5' tour organised by the RCTS on 13th May 1962. Featuring a unique pairing of 'Schools' class 4-4-0 No. 30925 *Cheltenham* from Basingstoke shed and ex-LMS 2P 4-4-0 No. 40646, the 9-coach special started and finished at Nottingham Victoria on a circular route taking in Wakefield, Harrogate, Ripon and Darlington and a return via York, Doncaster, and Newark. A 2-hour stop at York between 5-7pm was allowed for during the return leg. Rather alarmingly, after the tour it was reported that No. 40646 should not have worked as its boiler ticket had expired! Despite this and the 2P being considered as 'rough as old boots' by its crew, the two locos were said to have attained 'a sprightly run from Darlington to York' with a top speed of 83mph achieved at Thirsk. The 2P was promptly condemned on its return to its home shed at Bescot whereas 30925 survived after withdrawal in December 1962 to become a star attraction at the Mid-Hants Railway. *NS204514*

How are the mighty fallen! South of York at Chaloners Whin Junction, Peppercorn A1 4-6-2 No. 60145 (formerly named *Saint Mungo*) of Darlington shed passes with a Class K freight from Dringhouses yard to Healey Mills on 19 March 1966. Although bereft of nameplates, externally the loco looked as if someone still cared and at this date was one of only two survivors of the class, the other being No. 60124 *Kenilworth*. A cheery Neville Stead who was instrumental in arranging the loco for the duty is seen looking out from the cab. Both locos were withdrawn a week later but No. 60145 was reprieved and reinstated for further work based at York shed on 17th April. However, the end wasn't long in coming with final withdrawal occurring on 19th June 1966 and the cutters' torch at Drapers yard, Hull finished her off later in the year after a tragically short career of just 17 years 2 months. None of the class of 49 survived to be preserved although the class is now represented by the new build A1 No. 60163 *Tornado* completed in 2008. *NS204682*

Not to be forgotten is the role that York played as a museum prior to moving to its present location. The former boiler shop of the Y&NMR Works at Queen Street was selected in 1927 to house the very first museum after the 1925 Railway Centenary Exhibition held in York. After rebuffing a Beeching closure scheme, the terms of the 1968 Transport Act paved the way for a National Railway Museum to be set up at York as a branch of the Science Museum to house the expanding collection then also located in Clapham. The Queen Street Museum closed on 31st December 1973 and the collection temporarily moved to the former Leeman Road Goods Warehouse pending a final move to the new museum. Ex-L&YR 'Pug' 0-4-0ST No. 51235 had transferred to York from Burton shed in November 1956 and is seen on a temporary track about to move the GWR 4-4-0 *City of Truro* prior to the latter being restored for its period of main line running commencing in 1957. No. 51235 remained at York and was withdrawn in November 1958. *NS204503*

A striking portrait of two ex-NER Class X 4-8-0T's (LNER Class T1) No's 69910/16 awaiting further work at the throat of the York Main Goods lines in 1956. The view looks south-east towards York South loco sheds with the footbridge above connecting one of the Wagon Works buildings to the left with the Carriage Works out of sight on the right. The class of ten 3-cylinder locos designed by Wilson Worsdell was introduced between 1909-10 and a further five were built by the LNER in 1925 for heavy mineral duties between marshalling sidings in Durham and Yorkshire to port reception yards at Hull, Middlesbrough, and Tyne Dock. Both engines had arrived at York from Newport (Teesside) shed in October 1955 with No. 69916 staying until withdrawn in August 1957. No. 69910 moved to Selby for work at Gascoigne Wood sidings in November 1958 but returned to York in September 1959 only to be withdrawn the following month. *NS204932A*

THE DVLR

The 16 mile Derwent Valley Light Railway (DVLR) was opened in stages between 1912 and 1913 between Layerthorpe on the goods only Foss Island branch at York to Cliffe Common on the Selby to Market Weighton line. There were nine intermediate stations. The line remained privately operated throughout its life using NER and LNER locos to power the train services. Although built primarily for freight, a passenger service ran until 1926 and the line was also used as a diversionary route during the Great War. At Cliffe Common on 14th August 1959 J25 0-6-0 No. 65714 heads what is by this date the one remaining freight service 'out and back' from York. The York-based loco was used regularly on the line until its withdrawal in January 1961. Cliffe Common Station on the Selby line is just visible beyond the fence to the left of the loco. *NS201917*

On the DVLR on 29th February 1960 J25 No. 65714 is seen again, this time at the level crossing at Murton Lane station. The train consists of a very respectable payload heading east towards York having picked up consignments en route. BR closed the Selby to Driffield Line in 1964, thus cutting off the DVLR southern outlet connection at Cliffe Common. This was followed by the closure of the DVLR section south of Wheldrake in 1965, the next section north as far as Elvington in 1968 and then as far as Dunnington in 1973. A four mile section from Layerthorpe to Dunnington survived until 1981 when the traffic source at Dunnington Grain Drier was closed. The last freight ran on 22nd September 1981. A preserved ½ mile section of the line at Murton Lane survives as part of the Murton Park Yorkshire Museum of Farming and is operated by the DVLR Society. *JSCMH34*

THIRSK

The famous 44 mile 'racing' section between York and Darlington opened to passengers on 31st March 1841 and the section south of Thirsk became one of the favoured photographic locations to record trains at speed. The line south of Pilmoor to north of Thirsk was quadrupled in 1942 as a necessary wartime measure and, typifying this part of the route, A3 Pacific No. 60077 *The White Knight* of Heaton shed speeds south from Thirsk with an express on 21st May 1959. The loco was named after the winner of the 1907 and 1908 Ascot Gold Cup and was completed in October 1924. It had received a boiler replacement and a double chimney the previous month and 'German' (trough) deflectors were fitted in July 1961. From July 1963 it was based at Edinburgh St. Margarets shed and was withdrawn from there during July 1964. Thirsk Junction station is behind the Station Road bridge in the distance and the water tank seen on the left of the running lines marks the position of the long-closed (1930) Thirsk loco shed which sat in the 'V' of the junction of the Melmerby/Ripon line. *NS204577*

With steam to spare, during the early to mid-1950s, ex-NER Q6 0-8-0 No. 63419 passes under Station Road bridge at Thirsk with a southbound coal train comprising a mix of BR steel bodied 16 tonners and vintage wooden bodied wagons. The loco was completed in February 1920 by the Armstrong Whitworth Scotswood Works at Newcastle and had been based from 1937 at East Hartlepool shed until this was closed in April 1939 and the loco stock moved to West Hartlepool shed. Between 1942 and 1948 the loco was based at Newport (Teesside) shed before a final move back to West Hartlepool shed proved to be the last until withdrawal occurred in June 1965. The substantial building in the background was part of the GNER Thirsk Junction goods yard and coal depot accessed from the Up side of the line to the north of the station. *NS204588*

Thirsk station opened on 31st March 1841 on the GNER Darlington to York route. After the opening of the rival Leeds & Thirsk 'Town' terminus in 1848, the GNER station acquired the suffix 'Junction' but it never officially appeared as such in contemporary timetables. The unofficial title persisted even after the 'Town' station lost its scheduled passenger service in the 1850s and became a goods station. As the GNER station was a mile from the centre of town, a connecting bus service bridged the gap between the two and despite the inconvenience the GNER station proved useful to access the neighbouring racecourse on the main road into town. After quadrupling of the line in 1942 the two station platforms were revamped as island platforms with the long-distance fast services using the two inner faces and local services using the two outer faces. On 21st May 1959 V2 2-6-2 No. 60812 of Heaton shed passes through the station with an Up express while a gaggle of spotters record its passage. From 1945 the loco spent eighteen years at Heaton before finishing its career at Gateshead where withdrawal occurred in July 1964. *NS204587*

A rare and interesting photograph taken at Thirsk South Junction within the 'V' of the main line to York (on left) and the chord of the Leeds line via Melmerby and Ripon curving away to the right. Seen marshalling stock either before or after heading the Thirsk Town local pick-up service is J25 0-6-0 No. 65720, probably of Northallerton shed where she was based between January 1951 and December 1955 before moving to the Teesside area. In the background can be seen the two-road Thirsk shed dating from 1887 which at the time of the 1923 Grouping had an allocation of some fourteen locos including two of the large Class A7 4-6-2Ts. Although closed on 10th November 1930, it continued to function as a yard and watering point and remained until the site was cleared in 1965. The J25 finished her career at Thornaby shed, Middlesbrough, and was withdrawn in April 1962. *NS204589*

The Leeds & Thirsk Railway opened their 'Town' terminus to goods on 5th January 1848 and to passengers on 1st June 1848 having crossed over the GNER main line ½ mile to the south of Thirsk Junction station. A scheduled passenger service was maintained until late 1855/early 1856 after which all such services were diverted permanently to the GNER station; the Town terminus then becoming goods only. The goods facilities (excluding those for livestock which were dealt with at the main line station's yard) included warehousing, a coal depot with drops, a 5-ton capacity yard crane and until c.1855 even a two-road engine shed and turntable. In this capacity it survived until 3 October 1966 – a date which also applied to the cessation of goods services at the main line station. Riddles BR Class 2 2-6-0 No. 78010 is seen assembling a modest payload sometime during the 1950s when it was based at Northallerton shed. The building on the left is Bamlett's Agricultural Engineering Works founded next to the yard in 1860. *NS204591*

York's B16 4-6-0 No. 61456 darkens the sky as it powers dramatically through Pilmoor station with a Class C fitted freight comprising mostly of loaded container 'flat' wagons – a traffic in which BR invested heavily until the late 1950s when competition from road enterprises began to bite seriously. Pilmoor station opened on 20th September 1847 as the junction for the Boroughbridge branch and then in 1875 the extension to Knaresborough by which time the importance of Pilmoor had increased with connections to the Malton and Pickering lines. The station was rebuilt with a new main building and station master's house during 1942 when the main line was quadrupled but closure to passengers and goods occurred as from 5th May 1958 after passenger services had ceased earlier on the Knaresborough/Malton/Pickering lines. No. 61456 lasted a little longer and was withdrawn from York shed during August 1960. *NS201494*

At Pilmoor on 29th May 1950 push/pull fitted G5 0-4-4T No. 67337 of Starbeck shed has arrived with the return service from Harrogate via Boroughbridge and Knaresborough. The passenger service had barely four months to run before ceasing as from Monday 25th September with the last trains running on the previous Saturday. Trains on the last day were well patronised and hauled by No. 67337 and also Starbeck's non-push/pull fitted G5 No. 67289 which hauled the very last departure from Pilmoor to Harrogate. A residual goods service lingered on the line until 1964. No. 67337 subsequently gravitated to Hull and Middlesbrough and was withdrawn from the latter in March 1957. *OTA4558*

During the early to mid-1950s V2 2-6-2 No. 60821 passes under Station Lane Road bridge and surges through Beningbrough station with a Down express. This was the first station on the line 'out' from York and opened on 31st March 1841 but named then as 'Shipton' – a village lying ½ mile due east. On December 1st 1898 the name was changed to 'Beningbrough' possibly resulting from the influence of the Dawnay family, the owners of Beningbrough Hall. The attractive signal cabin dated from the 1933 widening and was an LNER Type 12 example of their 'modernist' style equipped with a Mackenzie & Holland No. 17 frame with 35 levers. Also of interest is the blast wall protecting the locking room door and the bricked up front locking room window – a WW2 modification. The station closed to passengers on 15th September 1958 and the signal cabin in November 1963 – the latter probably coinciding with the closure of the small goods yard and coal depot to the north of the station on the Down side of the line. The V2 was withdrawn from New England shed at the end of December 1962. *NS204577*

Scoop! Although slightly north of the geographic remit of this book, this rare shot of two A3s double heading 20 plus bogies at Otterington on Friday 27th March 1953 begs for inclusion! The train is the celebrated 9.20am Newcastle Scotswood Sidings – Holloway (North London) empty carriage stock working which ran every day from Monday to Saturday. Although combinations of A1/A3 Pacifics, B1 4-6-0s and V2 2-6-2s were recorded it was very unusual to see two A3s harnessed together to haul the train. No. 60086 *Gainsborough* was based at Leeds Neville Hill shed while No. 60075 *St. Frusquin* had arrived at Gateshead shed six days previously from Darlington shed. No. 60086 piloted the train from Stockton as far as Thirsk when it then headed for home with a Leeds-bound service. The loco was similarly employed on a number of occasions during March and April although as far as is known this was the only occasion it assisted a classmate. *NS206495*

THE EASINGWOLD RAILWAY

The 2½ mile Easingwold Railway which ran from a junction at Alne on the NER main line opened on 25th July 1891 and was the result of local landowners and residents banding together to acquire their own railway given the failure of earlier attempts. Although built before the passing of the 1896 Light Railway Act, the line and its operation was said to have provided a valuable template for working up the new legislation, but despite this it was not until 1928 that it was officially incorporated under the terms of the Act. As a private concern for its entire existence it managed to turn a profit and pay a regular dividend from around 1910 until 1931 after which date road competition, urgent infrastructure renewals and the need to hire locos from the LNER and BR all took their toll. As deficits increased the passenger service was ceased as from 29th November 1948 and the last freight service ran on 27th December 1957 hauled by York loanee J72 0-6-0T No. 68698 hauling a parcels van, two covered goods vans, three open wagons of sugar beet and an empty mineral wagon. In this delightful view taken in the very early BR period at the terminus, the driver of J71 0-6-0T No. 68294 looks as if he is setting off to replenish his billy can (and a quick pint at the Station Hotel?) while his steed percolates in front of an ex-Cheshire Lines Committee 6-wheel brake composite carriage. The latter replaced an NER carriage 4-wheeler in around 1946 and its position over the platform ramp suggests that it is not about to form a public service thus possibly dating the shot after the passenger service had ceased. *NS208812*

As a precursor to closure several rail tours visited the branch including the first major tour organised by the Branch Line Society on Sunday 2nd June 1957. This covered closed lines in Yorkshire including a trip over the Easingwold Railway in eight open wagons plus a parcels van hauled by Worsdell J72 0-6-0T No. 68726 of York shed. The train is seen at the terminus against the backdrop of the station building seen above the train and the 1892 Station Hotel to the left. The tiny, long-closed loco shed is also seen on the extreme right. Society members commented that although closure was only a few months away, traffic on the line seemed surprisingly good with at least a dozen goods wagons in the yard. Although the station was destroyed by fire in 1967 and the yard and other buildings demolished and cleared, the Station Hotel survives virtually unchanged as a private residence. *NS208814*

MALTON

The Y&NMR 42 mile Scarborough route was opened throughout on 7th July 1845 and along with six other intermediate stations on the 21 mile York-Malton section, Barton (the suffix 'Hill' was added in 1853), at 11½ miles from York, was opened at the same time. As with other stations on this section it closed to scheduled passenger services on 22nd September 1930 and finally to goods from 10th August 1964. Looking north-east from the A64 overbridge with Barton Hill seen in the left background, Worsdell's D20 4-4-0 No. 62374 approaches the station (which is behind the photographer) with a parcels/van service from Scarborough in the early 1950s. The D20 was built in October 1906 and along with other classmates was a long-term Selby shed resident regularly used on local services in the area. Helping to narrow the date of the photograph down slightly, No. 62374 was withdrawn in October 1954 at a time when Selby had six of the class on its books and were still performing smart work on local services plus summer excursions to the east coast seaside resorts.
NS201594

Top: On the northern section of the Malton route, the line followed the western side of the meandering River Derwent. Kirkham Abbey station opened in its picturesque valley location in July 1845 and was originally named just 'Kirkham' until June 1875 when the suffix 'Abbey' was added to embrace the nearby 12th Century Augustinian Priory on the eastern side of the river. York-based B16/3 4-6-0 No. 61418 passes over the level crossing and through the now closed to passengers (1930) station with a York-bound service on 29th July 1961. The loco was built in November 1920 and was the first of seventeen to be rebuilt as a 'B16/3' from 1944 with modifications to the valve gear and a change over to left hand drive. It was amongst the last of the class to be withdrawn during 1964. The station building (now a private residence) was separate to the platform and is seen above and to one side of the loco while the NER brick-built 'S1a' signal cabin dating from 1873 also survives and is now a Grade II listed building. The cabin was initially provided with a 13-lever Mackenzie & Holland frame later extended to 16 levers. *NS201422*

Bottom: The setting of the River Derwent, its bridge and the ruins of the priory are a delightful backdrop to Kirkham Abbey goods yard with York's J27 0-6-0 No. 65887 busily engaged shunting for a pick-up goods duty. Of interest is the bogie bolster wagon which will be used to carry the substantial tree trunks off for processing. The store of sawn timber seen above the boiler of the loco may also suggest there was a sawmilling capability here, but could equally suggest it was a reception point for processed timber brought in by rail. Although the photograph is undated, the loco spent ten years at York before moving to Sunderland shed in December 1961 where it was withdrawn in May 1963. Residual goods traffic on the York - Malton line was discontinued as from 10th August 1964. Monastic life at Kirkham Priory ended in December 1539 during Henry VIII's Dissolution of the Abbeys programme and the buildings sold off during the following year. The building fabric was gradually stripped during the ensuing years but enough was left for it to become cared for by the Office of Works in the 1920's and since February 1987 it is now Grade 1 listed with English Heritage. *NS201830*

Just ¾ mile to the north of Kirkham Abbey was Castle Howard station serving the village of Welburn and the baronial residence of the Howard family. To all intents and purposes the station was a private halt for the Howard family in return for granting estate land to the Y&NMR. As befitting an adjunct of the stately home the Y&NMR architect George Andrews incorporated a statement flourish of the Italianate into the station building design as can be seen in the photograph. After the station's closure to passengers in 1930, the redundant wooden waiting room on the Up platform was let as a holiday cottage until the 1950s. After the final closure of the station to goods in November 1959, the station building fell into a period of neglect until restoration work was commenced by a new owner in 1979 and continued by the current owner from 1986. The building is now Grade II listed. The signal box was demolished in 1979. LNER B1 4-6-0 No. 61218 from Neville Hill shed passes through the station with a Leeds - Scarborough service sometime during the 1950s. The platform nameboard (now finished in BR (NER) tangerine) survives at this date possibly for the benefit of those alighting from trains to use the holiday cottage. *NS201832*

On 8th June 1961 the Royal Train hauled by A4 Pacific No. 60028 *Walter K. Whigham* travelled from London King's Cross to York for the wedding of the Duke of Kent to Katharine Worsley at York Minster. Two other trains conveying wedding guests made the same journey hauled by A4s No. 60003 *Andrew K. McCosh* and No. 60015 *Quicksilver*. In addition, No. 60014 *Silver Link* acted as 'spare' engine, all of which (allegedly) left King's Cross shed short of power and needing to borrow locos from other sheds! After the service at York Minster, the royal party plus guests were conveyed to the bride's home at Hovingham Hall, near Malton, in a fleet of buses. In the meantime, the three A4s worked light engine to Malton (possibly after victualling on North shed) with the carriage stock for all three trains also taken there by alternative power (2 diesels and a V2 2-6-2 loco) to await the arrival of the royal party and guests from Hovingham Hall for the return to London via York. No. 60028 (with white cab roof) is seen late in the afternoon approaching Kirkham Abbey station on the return trip from Malton. *NS201845*

Top: A 1950s view of a very trim Malton station (surely a modeller's dream!) looking from the east end of the Island 'through' platforms towards York. The station was located on the southern bank of the River Derwent and opened on 7th July 1845. Most noticeable in this shot is the George Andrews-designed overall roof with a weather screen at the distant end and a full width platform canopy extending from the roof supporting wall. The bay platform for the Whitby and Driffield services is out of sight to the right under the canopy which extended behind the photographer. The main platform facilities are also seen to the right. Malton Station signal cabin is seen to the left and was one of three in the immediate area operational by the 1870s – East and West being the other two. The 'Station' cabin dated from 1873 and was an 'S1a' type with a Mackenzie & Holland 21-lever frame later extended to 55 levers in 1905. The cabin closed in May 1966. A feature of the platform operation until c.1966 was the solution adopted by the NER to allow passengers to access the island platform without recourse to a footbridge or boarded crossing. Instead, a movable section in the form of a wheeled trolley running on rails was installed and set at right-angles to the single running line. When the line was in use the trolley was wheeled back under the Up (York) platform and interlocked with the signals giving access to the platform. *NS201835*

Bottom: In this early 1950s view, the crew of LNER A8 4-6-2T No. 69882 of Whitby shed take time to smile for the photographer despite the rain while preparing to leave with a train for home. Originally one of a class of forty-five locos built by the NER as Class H1 4-4-4Ts between 1913 -21, the entire class was rebuilt by the LNER during the 1930s as 4-6-2Ts and reclassified 'A8'. No. 69882 was rebuilt in February 1936 (then numbered 1503) and spent much of the early 1950s gravitating between Neville Hill and Whitby sheds until moved from the latter in June 1956 to Hull Botanic Gardens shed. While at Whitby they proved to be capable performers on the challenging Scarborough – Middlesbrough coastal route until displaced by DMUs in the mid-1950s. No. 69882 survived until November 1958 when it was withdrawn from Thornaby shed. *NS201835A*

Malton loco shed, seen looking west on 5th April 1958, dated from 1853/4 but was extended in 1867 to house sufficient motive power for a network of cross-country branch services on the Driffield, Pilmoor, and Whitby lines. However, it seems not to have had responsibility for the York – Scarborough line other than goods services. In 1899 plans were drawn up for a roundhouse to be sited opposite the existing shed but these were not proceeded with. On view are resident ex-NER G5 0-4-4T No. 67248 and a snowplough-fitted J27 0-6-0 No. 65827 while J39 0-6-0 No. 64928 lurks in the background. The G5 was built in August 1894 and had arrived from Sunderland shed during early January 1958 and was not destined to see the year out, being withdrawn in December. The J27 had been transferred from York in February 1955 and remained at Malton until withdrawn in July 1959 as did the J39, withdrawn in July 1961. The shed became a victim of dieselisation plus the decline of freight traffic and closed on 15th April 1963. *NS201834*

On 26th August 1958 BR Standard Class 5 4-6-0 No. 73045 of Leeds Holbeck shed eases past Malton East signal cabin and approaches Malton station with what is probably the 12.38pm ex-Scarborough to York service – a duty on which it had regularly performed since the beginning of 1954. If the assumption is correct the loco will continue to Leeds with the next part of the duty - the 3.10pm 'empties' to Neville Hill and thence light engine to the shed. The loco arrived new at Holbeck from Derby Works in November 1953 and stayed until transferred to Leicester GCR shed in September 1959. The loco lasted until August 1967 when it was withdrawn from Patricroft shed where it had spent the last two years of its 13 year 9 month career. *NS201794*

Looking west towards Malton station also on 26th August 1958, LMS Ivatt Class 4MT 2-6-0 No. 43077 of Hull Dairycoates shed has just passed through the station with a Class K Hull to Scarborough pick-up goods service. With three other new classmates (Nos. 43076/8/9) the loco had arrived new from Derby Works to Dairycoates in October 1950 to replace time-expired ex-NER 0-6-0s and all stayed until 1965 with No. 43077 moving to Goole shed in August. More of the class arrived during 1951 until in 1954 the shed had fifteen on its books with these ranging far and wide on a variety of freight duties. The surviving NER lower quadrant arms seen 'pegged' for the train probably lasted until replacement became necessary or, more likely, when colour lights were installed and the track layout rationalised. Considered by many as the ugliest loco ever to run on British metals, the 162-strong, 2-cylinder class incorporated many features aimed to ease maintenance including high running-plates which tended to accentuate the motion and oddly placed cylinders below. Nicknamed 'doodlebugs' by railwaymen and more disparagingly 'flying pigs' or 'mucky ducks' by enthusiasts, only one of the class survived into preservation - No. 43106 now at work on the Severn Railway where it is a popular performer.' *NS201793*

MARKET WEIGHTON

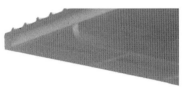

The Y&NMR threw out a lengthy 21½ mile tentacle from Bootham Junction on the York-Malton line to a terminus at Market Weighton in 1847. Despite the arrival of the Selby line in 1848 Market Weighton remained a terminus until 1865 when the line was extended to Beverley in May 1865 and to Driffield in 1890. On 1st May 1952 Gresley 3-cylinder D49 4-4-0 No. 62720 *Cambridgeshire* from Hull Botanic Gardens shed enters the station with a Hull - York stopping service. The loco was built in May 1928 and was just one of six of the 76-strong class built with oscillating cam-operated Lentz poppet valves – a troublesome arrangement which was replaced with new cylinders and piston valves during 1938. By the time of the photograph the class were increasingly being cascaded to secondary duties by large numbers of the Thompson B1 4-6-0 class – a process which accelerated with the introduction of DMUs. Withdrawals of the class started in earnest during 1957 with No. 62720 lasting until October 1959 after a long period at Botanic Gardens shed. *NS006731*

In the railway era Market Weighton was the meeting point of four separate routes and as such became known as the 'Crossroads of the Wolds' and even had its own loco shed and turntable until closed in 1917 as a wartime economy. It was also a focal point for many holiday season trains heading for the east coast resorts and one of these during the 1950s is headed by B1 4-6-0 No. 61276 which has left the station and is 'pegged' for the Driffield line at East Junction to either Bridlington, Filey or Scarborough. The loco arrived new to Darlington Bank Top shed in January 1948 and remained there until moved to York in June 1959 where it was withdrawn in June 1965. To the left of the train the goods shed with smoke exhaust damage to the roof (a good modeller's detail perhaps?) advertises the presence of G.T. Ripley, a local distributor of seed potatoes from Scotland and locally grown carrots. *NS200295*

Gresley K3 3-cylinder 2-6-0 No. 61902 approaches Market Weighton station with a service from Hull in the early 1960s. The loco is carrying a '50B' shedplate indicating Hull Dairycoates as its home shed at a time when there were more than twenty of the class based there. The class first appeared in 1920 and construction continued with internal variations until 1937 when a total of 193 had been completed. During the 1920s the class acquired the nickname 'Jazzers' by virtue of their syncopated exhaust beat and a trailing end gyration said to resemble the sound and movement of jazz music! Although the class was originally intended for fast goods work, the locos quickly became regarded as 'maids of all work' performers capable of hauling virtually anything on any route but did have an unenviable reputation for rough riding – especially when becoming overdue for a works visit. No. 61902 was new to traffic in July 1934 and from 1948 spent the rest of its career at Hull Dairycoates shed until withdrawn in September 1961. *NS200301*

On 6th March 1965 the preserved Gresley K4 2-6-0 No. 3442 *The Great Marquess* paused at Market Weighton with the SLS/MLS 'Whitby Moors Rail Tour'. The trip started at Manchester Victoria with No. 3442 replacing Jubilee 4-6-0 No. 45698 *Mars* at Wakefield Kirkgate before moving on to Market Weighton where K1 2-6-0 No. 62005 was attached for the continuation of the trip to Scarborough and Whitby. The return to Manchester was via Malton and York where the K1 came off leaving No. 3442 to run to Wakefield where the Jubilee came on and completed the return to Manchester. The train is seen at Market Weighton where tour passengers make the most of the stop to take photographs prior to the attachment of the K1. The station had an overall roof until 1947/8 when it was replaced by platform awnings. All four of the routes which passed through Market Weighton became victims of the Beeching 'Reshaping' plan with the last being the Beverley-York line; the closure of which from 29 November 1965 also saw the complete closure of Market Weighton station. *NS200300*

Warthill was the second Y&NMR station 'out' from York on the Market Weighton line and was originally named Stockton, then successively changed to Stockton Forest then Stockton-on-Forest and finally Warthill (a village about 1½ miles away!) in 1872. The station had two facing platforms, a generous 2-storey station building incorporating the station master's accommodation, a 2-storey crossing keeper's house, an 1880s NER Type S1a brick-built 15-lever (later 21) signal cabin and a goods yard with three sidings and coal drops. Between 1922 and 1932 Warthill was also the terminus of the 1ft 6in gauge 5¼ mile Sand Hutton Light Railway. D49 4-4-0 No. 62717 *Banffshire* of Hull Botanic Gardens shed heads a York-bound service through the station and level crossing sometime in the 1950s. Although the photograph is undated, the level crossing has a set of lifting boom barriers which replaced the manually-operated gates in 1952 and were the first to be installed in Britain. DMUs were introduced on the line in 1957 and Warthill closed to passengers as from 5th January 1959 and to goods on 7th June 1965 but fortunately all three buildings mentioned survive today in residential use. The D49 was withdrawn from Hull Dairycoates shed in January 1961 – the year that saw the last fourteen of the class also succumb. *NS206705*

SELBY

Selby has the distinction of being the first station in Yorkshire when opened by the Leeds & Selby Railway on 22nd September 1834. The original station (a terminus by the banks of the River Ouse) was superseded by the opening of the Hull & Selby on 1st July 1840 and a new through station which was successively rebuilt in 1873 and 1891. By the latter date Selby had become the confluence of six lines thereby creating an important junction for services to the north, south, east, and west – a position which it maintains to this day. Ex-NER D20 4-4-0 No. 62384 is seen departing north from the station on 28th August 1952 during a period when Selby's allocation of six of the class were doing good work on Doncaster/Harrogate/Hull/Leeds/York services plus summer specials to Bridlington, Filey and Scarborough. Apart from two short spells at Starbeck shed the loco spent all of its BR career at Selby shed until withdrawn in August 1955. The signal bridge is worthy of note because the NER lower quadrant upper arms have been replaced with upper quadrant arms, but the repeaters below retain the lower quadrant arms thus giving an unusual aspect when pulled off with one arm 'up' and one 'down'. The station was Grade II listed in 1980. *NS200117A*

On 29th October 1954 Heaton's A2/3 Pacific No. 60511 *Airborne* (named after the winner of the 1946 Derby and St Leger races) passes through the station's Up through road with an express. The loco was built in July 1946 and was one of the forty-five Pacifics authorised for the 1945/6 building programme during Edward Thompson's LNER regime. No. 511 was one of the first batch of fifteen produced up to September 1947 and reflective of his drive for simplification and standardisation. However, after Thompson's retirement in July 1946 his successor, Arthur Peppercorn, chose to incorporate his own design features into the remainder of the design once the first fifteen had entered traffic. No. 60511 was based at Heaton until October 1961 when it was moved to Tweedmouth shed to cover goods workings and main line failures, lasting there until withdrawn to store at the end of the '62 summer timetable and finally condemned in November the same year. In the background and on its gantry over the tracks is the 1891 Selby swing bridge signal cabin which controlled the river traffic below. *NS200112*

At the north end of Selby station Doncaster-based V2 2-6-2 No. 60872 *King's Own Yorkshire Light Infantry* waits to depart on 28th March 1959. Completed in April 1939, it was one of the class named after four army regiments and two schools with close connections with the north-east of England. No. 60872 (then numbered 4843) was named at Doncaster Works on 20th May 1939 with Lady Deedes, the wife of the Regiment's Colonel, Sir Charles P. Deedes, performing the ceremony. The regimental badge consisting of a bugle horn surrounding the white rose of York, the motto *Cede Nullis* (surrender to none) below a royal crown was added below the nameplate script. But for the outbreak of WW2 it is thought that more names would have been awarded to other members of the class. Fittingly, on 30th December 1961 the loco was recorded hauling an 11-coach troop special for the regiment on part of the journey from Pontefract to Southampton where it embarked for Malaya. This fine loco remained at Doncaster until it did 'surrender' (along with eleven others of the class) to withdrawal on 22nd September 1963 by which time it had lost its nameplate. It was cut up during the following month. *NS208089*

Ex-GCR Robinson 'Pom-Pom' J11 0-6-0 No. 64419 arrives at Selby on 20th June 1954 with the Sheffield branch of the RCTS 'South Yorkshire Rail Tour No. 3'. The tour, chalked up as '944', started at Sheffield Midland with No. 64419 from Sheffield Darnall shed in charge of the first two legs of the tour taking in Rotherham and Scunthorpe before handing over at Selby to J21 0-6-0 No. 65078 of Darlington shed. This loco then took the tour on to York via the DVLR. The return to Sheffield was headed by York's V2 2-6-2 No. 60847 *St. Peter's School York, A.D. 627*. The interesting scene at Selby is at approx. 4.45pm with the J11 about to give way to the J21 which will depart at around 5pm for the trip along the DVLR from Cliffe Common. The J11 experienced problems en route from Sheffield and needed attention at Frodingham shed before proceeding on to Selby which was reached some 42 minutes late - no wonder she is looking a little 'tired'! The loco nevertheless soldiered on until August 1962 while the J21 finished at Tweedmouth where it was condemned in March 1957. *NS200120*

At the south end of Selby station in 1950 G5 0-4-4T No. 67250 is marshalling the stock for the Goole push/pull service – a regular duty for the Selby-based loco until withdrawn in September 1957. At much the same time DMUs replaced the steam-hauled stock until the service itself was discontinued in June 1964. The coaching stock seen in the photograph comprises a standard LNER brake third and a 12-wheel GCR saloon – possibly employed here as the 'driver trailer'. The G5 was push/pull fitted in November 1940 – one of twenty-one so fitted between 1939 and 1951. Of interest is the signal bridge which has additional arms added by means of a unique underslung gantry which may have given extra strengthening for the main structure. A local user of the push/pull service observed that the carriages remained in the LNER teak livery until well into the 1950s. *NS200122A*

On 17th August 1961 the northbound 'Elizabethan' express coasts through Selby hauled by immaculate King's Cross A4 Pacific No. 60030 *Golden Fleece.*
This was the last summer the train was worked by steam – an event originally intended for 1960 but postponed because of the lack of diesel power to cover
the 1961 summer services. As numbered 4495 when completed in August 1937, the loco briefly appeared named as *Great Snipe* but a change of policy
moving away from bird names saw it go back into the Doncaster Paint Shop finished in green on 12th September to reappear blue and nameless six days
later and then in the following week receive its *Golden Fleece* nameplates. The loco is photographed fresh from her 46-day 'General' overhaul at Doncaster
the previous month when a speedometer was also fitted. This would prove to be her last major works visit before withdrawal with four other King's Cross
classmates in December 1962. *NS200133*

Away from the glamour of main line activities, on 22nd August 1958 Sentinel Y1 0-4-0T No. 68150 shunts three tanker wagons at the British Oil & Cake Mill (BOCM) mills to the north of Selby. The mills spanned both sides of the Hull line near Barlby Junction and were one of Selby's largest employers with buildings dominating the River Ouse 'Long Reach' waterfront. The single-geared Y1 dated from August 1929 (then numbered as '183') and was first employed at Gateshead and Malton before arriving at Selby in June 1954 mainly for work in the smaller yards and the BOCM sidings. The loco arrived at more or less the same time as double-geared Y3 0-4-0T No. 68180 from Gateshead as replacements for withdrawn classmates No. 68143 and Y3 0-4-0T No. 68156. Withdrawal of No. 68150 at Selby occurred in May 1959 just four months before the closure of the shed itself. *NS206381*

Selby's engine shed dated from 1871 and was sited south of the station in the 'V' of the junction of the Doncaster and Leeds lines. Designed by Thomas Prosser, the NER Chief Architect from 1854-74, the shed was a standard roundhouse within a square building with 18 stalls and 2 access roads radiating from a central 42ft turntable. An adjoining and similar structure designed by William Bell, the Chief Architect from 1877-1914, was added in 1898 with 22 stalls and 2 access roads grouped around a 50ft turntable. By 1923 the allocation stood at around 56 locos – a figure which had hardly changed thirty years later and still dominated by loco types used to shift coal from the South Yorkshire collieries. The LNER considered the shed important enough for a mechanical coaling plant which was installed in 1931. Seen grouped homogenously around one of the roundhouse turntables on 22nd August 1959 – just three weeks before the shed closed on 13 September - is a trio of J39 0-6-0s - from left to right - Nos. 64938, 64904 and 64860. Two were Selby locos (No. 64938 was from Malton shed) and all three were shortly to move on to other sheds in the Region. *NS208399*

Above: The church of St. James the Apostle, Selby, overlooks B16 4-6-0s Nos. 61432 and (probably) 61473 which on 16th June 1951 are either coming off shed or entering it from the Leeds line. Both locos were based at Neville Hill shed at this time when the class (apart from a couple at Scarborough) were equally divided between Leeds and York. Both locos remained in original condition throughout their careers and were withdrawn within a couple of months of one another with No. 61432 going from Neville Hill in July 1961 and No. 61473 from York in September 1961. Also seen is J71 0-6-0T No. 68235 which was used on the Cawood branch goods services until transferred to West Auckland shed in June 1958. The tower of the church was the scene of a tragic accident in 1944 when a Halifax bomber returning from a training flight crashed into the spire killing all seven of the crew and six local residents. The tower was rebuilt but without a spire. *AF0240*

Bottom: Sentinel Steam Railcars first appeared in the North-East during 1927 and imaginatively were given names of pre-railway age stage coaches. Two were allocated to Selby in 1927 for local services to Cawood, Goole, Staddlethorpe (on the Hull line) and York. The 6-cylinder 100hp car No. 2136 *Hope* was delivered new to Pickering in late 1928 but by 1947 it was the last of three operational units at Selby - the others being No. 2135 *Integrity* and No. 2267 *Recovery*. Towards the end *Hope* had been used on the Goole service with five weekday return trips and six on Saturdays. On withdrawal on 14th February 1948 (while nominally allocated to Whitby) it was the last Sentinel car remaining in service and the only one to become BR property. Seen at Selby after withdrawal, it awaits removal to Darlington for scrapping. *NS207579*

CHURCH FENTON

The Y&NMR line between York and Church Fenton opened with three intermediate stations (Copmanthorpe, Bolton Percy and Ulleskelf) on 29th May 1839 with the continuation to Milford Junction opening the following year. From 1871 the Selby line joined the Church Fenton line at Chaloners Whin Junction. Just to the north of the junction a minor road off the A64 at Dringhouses crossed the line, offering a handy photographic location, and from here looking north towards York B16 4-6-0 No. 61443 is seen approaching the junction with a lengthy and typically heterogeneous Class H freight on 6th October 1956. In common with many of its classmates the loco remained unrebuilt and spent the last nine years of its career based at York and was withdrawn in September 1961. *NS201469*

Near Copmanthorpe on 18th August 1931 the experimental Gresley W1 No. 10000 is seen on one of its many test runs after yet another visit to Darlington Works. When completed in November 1929 (it finally entered traffic in June 1930) it was the only 4-6-2-2 (but officially regarded as a 4-6-4) tender loco ever to run in Britain and had many innovative features: these including a Marine-type Yarrow Water-Tube boiler, a high working pressure of 450psi. and four cylinders for compound working. Because of the secrecy which shrouded the initial project since its birth in 1924 the loco was dubbed 'Hush-Hush', a name which stuck throughout its career. Although it was usually regarded a failure, it did haul a number of important trains with moderate success before being rebuilt completely with a conventional boiler and A4 streamlining in 1937. Tellingly, over a career span of 1,888 days since it entered traffic in its original condition, it had spent 1,105 days in Darlington Works! The loco retained its number under the Thompson 1943 renumbering scheme and became BR No. 60700 which it retained until withdrawal from Doncaster shed in June 1959. *NS207054*

Ulleskelf station, 8¾ miles from York, served the nearby village of the same name which derives from the Scandinavian personal name Úlfr and the Old English word 'skelf' for a flat area. As far as is known the station was originally a conventional 2-platformed installation until the NER quadrupling in 1903 caused a rebuild to an island platform set between the slow lines as seen in the photograph. The quadrupling also appears to have resulted in the replacement of the level crossing with a road bridge and the removal of the goods yard and signal box from the north of the station to the south. On 6th October 1956 LMS Black 5 4-6-0 No.44666 from Saltley shed passes through the very attractive station with a stopping service from York to Leeds. Fortunately, the station avoided the Beeching 'reshaping' axe due to the poor road network in the area and, although now unstaffed, remains open for business. *NS201922A*

After 1839 Church Fenton station assumed more importance with the opening of the Y&NMR line to Harrogate via Wetherby in 1848 and in 1869 with the NER link to Micklefield on the Leeds and Selby line. However, it lost its 'East Coast Main Line' status when the Doncaster – York line via Selby was opened in 1871. The line to York was quadrupled in 1903 to handle the increased traffic levels and in conjunction with this work an enlarged station with extra platforms was resited slightly to the south (back to its original 1839 site!) and opened in September 1904. In May 1952 K3 No. 61841 from March shed enters the station from the York line with a southbound Class H freight. The loco entered traffic in February 1925 and survived until withdrawn from Woodford Halse shed in March 1962. Also, of interest is one of the LNER station wooden nameboards which were not replaced by BR totems but were said to have survived until replaced by 1970s style corporate signage. *NS202000*

Another York-based B16 4-6-0 in original condition – this time No. 61426 – passes through the station with a northbound Class H freight in March 1952. The loco remained unrebuilt and was the second of the class to be withdrawn in September 1959 after the first (No. 61474) had gone in January 1958. At this time the three attractive station platform canopy awnings with side screens appear to be in the process of having most, if not all, of their glass replaced. Unfortunately, all three were removed during 1990 and replaced by utilitarian 'bus shelters'. *NS201435*

HARROGATE

The station at Knaresborough was opened by the Y&NMR on 1st October 1851 and replaced a temporary structure to the east of the town opened by the E&WYJR in October 1848 as a consequence of the collapse of the viaduct over the River Nidd on 11th March 1848. In 1865 the NER rebuilt the station to a design by their chief architect Thomas Prosser and there was a further rebuild in 1890 resulting in the fine structure as seen on 21st September 1958 looking north-east from the level crossing to the tunnel running under the High Street. The building was Grade II listed in 1986 and, although now unstaffed, the buildings on the eastbound platform are in private commercial use with one now tastefully restored as 'The Old Ticket Office' café in the former booking office. *BHF*

An undated, but unusual shot of the south tunnel portal at Knaresborough with D49 4-4-0 No. 62702 *Oxfordshire* appearing into the sunlight with a train probably from York and bound for Leeds. The loco was completed at Darlington in November 1927 and based at York throughout the 1950s until despatched briefly to Neville Hill shed in September 1958 where it was withdrawn two months later – one of thirty of the class disposed of that year. The tunnel portal with faux machicolations dated from 1851 and the similarly dated water tower seen on the left were both Grade II listed in 1985 and 1999 respectively. Unfortunately, the castellated structure to the right is no longer part of the scene.

After the collapse of the first viaduct over the River Nidd on 11th March 1848, work on its replacement commenced immediately afterwards and was completed by 1st October 1851 ready for the opening of the line through to Harrogate. The finished work cost almost £10,000 (almost £1.5m in today's money), stood 78ft above the river and was embellished with castellated parapets and piers to blend with the nearby medieval ruins of Knaresborough Castle. In May 1968 the viaduct was Grade II listed. Looking north upriver, on 24th April 1976 ex-L&NWR 'Jumbo' 2-4-0 No. 790 *Hardwicke* and ex-MR 'Compound' 4-4-0 No. 1000 head the Gainsborough Model Railway Society's 'London & North Western & Midland Railways Joint Tour' across the viaduct on the outward leg of the tour from York to Carnforth via Leeds. The tour returned to York via Hellifield hauled by A3 Pacific 4472 *Flying Scotsman*. Seen above the last two visible windows of the second carriage is Knaresborough station's 12-lever signal cabin – a most unusual non-standard stone structure built between 1871-3 as an addition to a row of existing properties. *NS2004566A*

Starbeck's loco shed originated in the late 1850s as a 2-road arched gable end slated roof building which was progressively extended in 1864, 1877, 1888 and 1889 to become the longest of its type in Britain. By 1956 the shed roof was in an appalling state and in the same year BR rebuilt it with brick screen walls, a flat roof and also reduced it in length as seen here on 12th September 1959 - just one day before it closed, and the existing stock (21) transferred elsewhere. The shed's allocation once totalled over 50 locos in the 1930s and became synonymous for its allocation of D49 4-4-0s – two of which are seen here – No. 62759 *The Craven*, which moved to Hull Dairycoates shed until withdrawn in January 1961, and No. 62738 *The Zetland* which moved to York only to be withdrawn the following week. Also seen is J39 0-6-0 No. 64861 which ended its career at Neville Hill shed in December 1962 and ex-LMS 3F 'Jinty' 0-6-0T No. 47462 which survived at Goole shed until September 1961. *NS208471*

The NER station at Harrogate opened on 1st August 1862 and replaced the 1848 Y&NMR Brunswick station located to the south of the town. At that date the station had become a confluence of five routes: from Crimple Junction to the south two lines diverging to Leeds via Arthington and Wetherby, to the north at Dragon Junction, two lines diverging to Northallerton via Ripon and to York via Knaresborough and lastly the branch line to Pateley Bridge diverging off the Ripon line at Ripley Junction. Starbeck's D49 4-4-0 No. 62738 *The Zetland* is seen again – this time at the station on 24th April 1957 in a happier state heading an Up stopping train for the south – probably Leeds. The train is already 'pegged' to leave by the underslung platform 4 starter signal – a similar but cantilevered arrangement for sighting purposes is seen projecting out from platform 5 on the left. Although the station appears to have two through lines there is only one as that nearest the train is a siding for stabling stock. *NS206837*

Ivatt GNR C1 Atlantic No. 4456 swings into Harrogate with a stopping service probably from Darlington or York to Leeds. The photograph may date from 18th July 1938 when similar shots were taken at this location. The loco was built in October 1910 and was one of the last batch of ten fitted with piston valves, Schmidt superheaters and with an increase in cylinder size from 18.75in to 20in. During LNER days the 32-element Robinson superheater was fitted to many of the class (No. 4456 got hers in May 1927) which greatly improved performances. The loco spent much of its LNER career based at Doncaster and is here probably fulfilling a 'triangular' duty which took it back home. With lack of maintenance and spares taking their toll during WW2, withdrawals began to bite from 1943 and many of the class were in a deplorable condition by the end of the conflict - plus their ranks were further eroded by the influx of the new B1 4-6-0s. No. 4456 managed to hang on long enough to receive its 1946 number (2886) but only lasted until August 1947 when it was withdrawn. Also of note is the NER splitter signal with slotted posts which probably survived until the new Harrogate North signal box opened in 1947. *NS202341*

The southbound 'Queen of Scots' Pullman express pulls away from its Harrogate stop on 22nd May 1959 hauled by A3 Pacific No. 60084 *Trigo* of Neville Hill shed. The service originated in 1923 as the 'Harrogate Pullman', but on 1st May 1928 its path was extended to Glasgow Queen Street station and it was renamed the 'Queen of Scots'. The train ran each weekday and Saturdays departing from King's Cross at 12 noon with an arrival at Glasgow (via Darlington, Newcastle, and Edinburgh) at around 9pm. The return service left Queen Street at 11am. Neville Hill supplied locos for the Harrogate – Newcastle leg of the journey and *Trigo* (named after the 1929 winner of the St Leger and Derby races) had been based there since September 1949, remaining there until moved to Gateshead in late 1963 where it was withdrawn in November 1964. *NS204569*

At the south end of Harrogate station and underneath the Station Road bridge, Riddles 'Standard 4' 2-6-4T No. 80120 of Neville Hill shed waits to depart with a Leeds train. With four others of the class the loco had gone new to Whitby shed in 1955 for work on the Scarborough services and then in June 1958 had moved to Neville Hill to work with B1 and B16 4-6-0s to replace withdrawn D49 4-4-0s. From November 1963 the loco gravitated north to Carstairs shed and then saw the finale of Scottish steam whilst based at Polmadie shed where it was withdrawn in May 1967. *NS204567*

Easter Monday in 1955 fell on April 11th and brought large crowds out to Wetherby races and also to Knaresborough and Harrogate – all needing a string of specials mostly run out from Leeds. Most unusually, ex-GNR Ivatt N1 0-6-2T No. 69484 from Leeds Ardsley shed was also roped in to haul a 5-coach special seen arriving at Harrogate that day. The loco was built in June 1912 with condensing gear for inner London suburban services and also transfer trips to South London. From the 1930s the class drifted out to West Riding sheds – a move which saw the loco become an émigré from Hatfield shed to Ardsley in 1951 when it probably lost its condensing gear. It remained at Ardsley until withdrawn in September 1957. *NS204568*

The impressive proportions of Starbeck's A6 4-6-2T No. 69791 are seen to good effect under the water crane at the north end of Harrogate station on 29th May 1950. The loco is fresh from a lengthy overhaul at Darlington and was the first of the class to receive a BR lined out livery and very smart she looks too. Vincent Raven built the class of ten between 1907 - 8 specifically to work the challenging Scarborough- Whitby coast line and all were originally 4-6-0Ts before being rebuilt as 4-6-2Ts with longer frames and larger coal and water capacities between 1914 -17. By the 1940s the class had drifted away from their coastal haunts and No. 69791 (still with its original Westinghouse brake and NER smokebox door) had been at Starbeck since March 1945 where she was used for local goods and piloting work plus occasional passenger services to Leeds. In February 1951 she was moved to Hull Botanic Gardens shed where withdrawal caught up with her in August 1951. In the background is the Pullman Kitchen Car *Joan* forming part of the 'Yorkshire Pullman' service from London King's Cross to Harrogate with a through portion to Hull. *NS204955*